Develop the Keys to Successful Living

LYDIA ANTI

iUniverse, Inc.
New York Bloomington

Develop the Keys to Successful Living

iUniverse books may be ordered through booksellers or by contacting:

iUniverse
1663 Liberty Drive
Bloomington, IN 47403
www.iuniverse.com
1-800-Authors (1-800-288-4677)

Because of the dynamic nature of the Internet, any Web addresses or links contained in this book may have changed since publication and may no longer be valid. The views expressed in this work are solely those of the author and do not necessarily reflect the views of the publisher, and the publisher hereby disclaims any responsibility for them.

ISBN: 978-1-4502-6195-1 (pbk)
ISBN: 978-1-4502-6196-8 (ebk)

Printed in the United States of America

iUniverse rev. date: 11/10/10

DEDICATION

This book is dedicated to my entire family whose names I have not mentioned. Special thanks go to my mum and dad Alice and Samuel Anti, who sacrificed their own happiness by putting me first to enable me to have a better life. To my siblings Endora Agyeman, William Anti, Florence Adu, Samuel Boadu, Doris Anti and Prince Adu my nephew. I am very thankful for all your support and encouragement which has made me what I am today. My best wishes to my brother Jackson Anti whose miraculous healing inspired me to write this book. "I am loved by you all not because I am perfect but because I am blessed".

Contents

INTRODUCTION

Are You A Doer or a Dreamer?

"Success seems to be connected with action. Successful men keep moving. They make mistakes, but they don't quit."
                                                                            —Conrad Hilton

In life, there are two categories of people: the dreamers and the achievers. Dreamers dream of how they will one day be successful, but they never take the necessary steps to make their dreams become a reality.

Achievers, on the other hand, make an effort to look for the right people who can help make their dreams come true. They take the necessary steps to achieve their dreams by seeking and gathering information in the right places to enable their dreams to flourish. Achievers become successful people; they get things done, and in doing so, they make things happen.

In this book, I will show you how to develop your abilities, talents, and skills and challenge you to look at some of your daily practices in all areas of your life, which might include habits that could affect you on your pathway to success. In addition to showing you how to identify your positive and negative habits, this book will present the necessary steps you can take to rectify some of the negative habits and turn them into positive ones for your own highest good.

The real-life situations that you will read about in this book are from an entire life's worth of experiences and observation of other people's mistakes, which I reflected on and then applied the knowledge I gained as I decided to change my life for the better and enable myself to be a success.

Discussed in this book are some of the most common and practical mistakes that people make on a daily basis. This book therefore serves as a positive way forward for any ambitious person who is willing to look at his or her life in general, apply the knowledge he or she gains from reading it, and use the principles presented to be a better person.

I have been in management for five years. I started work as a cleaner. I became a kitchen porter, a carer, a senior carer, and then a support worker and rose through the ranks to my current management position. Presently, I work with vulnerable adults with learning disabilities.

"You have the right to dream, but you have no right to anything you have not worked for."
                                                                            —Marian Wright Edelman

CHAPTER 1

Be Diligent

Do your tasks efficiently when at work, as that can open doors of opportunities which will enable you to get to the next level in your career development. It will help your manager have confidence in you and confidence that the work will be done when you are on duty.

As an employer and a manager at a care home for people with learning disabilities, one of my duties and responsibilities is to delegate tasks to the members of the team to ensure the smooth running of the home. Observing the work patterns of team members has exposed me to the different ways members of the team work.

There are various types of workers. There are the hard workers who give 100 percent when they are on duty. Then there are the workers who do their work but do not put in any extra effort. If you try to give these workers a bit of responsibility, they refuse and say it is not their job. Finally, there are the workers who need constant prompting or they will derail everything.

Do you want to attain a promotion at work? Start by showing up on time. Taking on extra tasks and completing them satisfactorily will draw your manager's attention to you. Your manager will realize you are pulling your weight. When the time for a promotion comes, who do you think your manager will promote? You, of course! You have earned the opportunity to be promoted through your hard work, so you deserve what you get.

When I worked at a corporation, I gave my best. I was diligent with my work. I followed the work ethic outlined in the Bible. I took the ant episode in the Bible seriously. The Bible advises us to go to the ant and learn from it. "Go to the ant, you lazybones; consider its ways, and be wise" (Proverbs 6:6).

Though I had only been in the post for six months, guess who the new position went to when my manager was asked to manage another project in the organization. Me, of course! I knew that I had earned it.

Robert Schuller says, "Bloom where you are planted." I did.

Let me explain the story of the ant to you so you will have a better understanding of the point I am making. The ant is a very small insect, but it is very wise. As small as it is, the ant is able to dig a hole deep into the ground. In summer, when the sun is high and the weather is good, because it knows that it is a tiny creature and it will take it a long time to gather enough food to last it through the winter months, it starts storing its food. In so doing, the ant painstakingly, bit by bit, takes a lot of food into its hole, enough to last it the entire winter. The Bible uses this illustration in Proverbs 6:6 when it asks the fool to go to the ant to learn its ways. It means people must learn wisdom and make good use of the moment and the available resources. People should learn to save for a rainy day or learn to change their lives for the better.

It is funny when a diligent employee gets promoted and the lazy ones or the ones who do their work but will not go the extra mile get jealous of the one who has put in the effort in his or her work.

As the old saying goes, "If wishes were horses, beggars would ride." You can wish all you like for success, but it will never come to you on a silver platter. You have to work for it. I have never met a successful person who is lazy.

A little bit better with your work contributes in making all the difference in getting the success you need.

All of us were born with the divine knowledge to discern right from wrong and the knowledge of what to do to achieve our dreams, but some just decide to do what they prefer because they do not want to pay the price. You see, unless you are born rich, there is always a price to pay to attain what you want. Some people want the crown, but they do not want the cross. However, the crown always comes with a cross.

Having lived over a score and ten, I have seen people wanting positions they have not worked hard for. If you do not prepare yourself for a higher position, how on earth do you expect to get such a post? The employer will only employ the qualified person, not the unqualified. Besides, what sort of skills have you acquired to tackle issues head-on when they raise their ugly heads? Positions come with responsibilities, and you have to acquire the necessary skills to be able to function effectively and efficiently.

"You will never reach the palace talking like a peasant." —Dr. Mike Murdock[1]

One has to prepare oneself by acquiring the necessary skills and abilities for the specific job one desires.

---

1   In *One Minute Businesswoman's Devotional*.

CHAPTER 2

Small Steps to Big Changes

The little things we do in life contribute a lot to our success or failure. Successful people do not take anything for granted, because little things accumulate into big things.

Think of all the little things we don't pay any attention to. Say an obese woman wants to lose weight. She knows she needs to watch what she eats, but she doesn't. She eats high-calorie foods, the very thing that will make her fat. A little thing like going for a walk might make a big difference for her too, but she doesn't do it. Instead, she sits in front of the television. She doesn't go to the gym. She doesn't exercise. Surprise! She piles on the pounds. Then she moans, "I'm fat."

Start by writing down your priorities. Then decide what little steps you can take to make them happen. What would you like to put right in your life? What have you done about it? What steps have you taken? For example, have you obtained information to reach your desired goal?

Let's get started with a few "little things" you can do now to change your life in a big way.

- Encourage someone who is down, as it can lift that person's mood.
- Smile at someone. This should make the person smile back. It could make his or her day that someone cared.
- Be polite on the phone.
- Accept responsibility for your actions; it shapes you for a better future.
- Be forgiving.

"Temper justice with mercy." —William Shakespeare

That is what little things can do.

CHAPTER 3

How's Your Attitude?

Attitude contributes a lot to an individual's development and success in life. I have seen people with the highest of qualifications, PhDs and other degrees, but because of their attitude, they work in an organization but never develop.

These people have more educational degrees than their bosses and thus act superior and are disrespectful. However, they forget it is the same manager they disrespect who may present them in a positive light and reveal their potential to senior management in the organization, which can lead to their promotion. It may also lead to being shortlisted when they apply for another vacancy within the same organization. It is also this same manager who will give them a reference when they leave the organization.

Your intelligence, knowledge, skills, and academic qualifications will take you to the palace, but your attitude will determine whether the king will enjoy your presence daily or throw you out of his court. A good attitude will open doors and obtain divine favor. God plays his part by opening a door for you in the form of a job, but it is your responsibility to apply for it, prepare for the interview, and get the job. Above all, your attitude will determine whether you are promoted or remain where you are.

Be Competent!

Although a good attitude can open doors, you need to be competent in your field of work. In fact, you need both competence and a good attitude to be efficient in your chosen field. There are some job opportunities that require you to acquire a university qualification. For example, before you can practice in the medical field in the capacity of a medical doctor, you need to attend medical school and obtain a medical degree and the appropriate licenses. If you want to be a specialist in computer information systems, you need to study for the appropriate qualifications that come in the form of degrees or professional certifications, so you can put what you have learned into practice to gain experience. Certain types of work require high academic learning. In such a situation, your attitude alone is not enough. You need the necessary qualifications and the experience to be able to do the job effectively.

> "If you think you can do something, that's confidence. If you can do it, that's competence. Both are needed for success." —John Maxwell, *The Difference Maker*

CHAPTER 4

Your Words Can Make You or Break You

Have you ever had an experience in which a very good friend all of a sudden stops seeking your company and phoning you? Did you ask yourself if you'd said something to offend her? Did you wonder if you touched something you shouldn't have or betrayed her trust? Did you gossip about her? Think about it, and you'll know what you did, won't you? You see, a lot of questions answer our worries. What I'm trying to say is that you cannot go talking horribly about people and expect them to be friendly toward you. It is possible you alienated your friend through your inability to control your tongue. In the same way, word reached your boss about something insensitive that you said about her, and she has started picking on your vulnerable areas in your job.

Take a close look at your professional relationships. Be honest! Are you all of a sudden having a hard time with your colleagues or your boss? Could it possibly be something insensitive or cruel you've said? Were you a gossip? Were you unsupportive of a colleague? Ask yourself questions, and you will find the answer. As the Bible states in Proverbs 6:2, "You are snared by the utterance of your lips; caught by the words of your mouth."

One of my best friends is Jamaican, and she has a cloth sign hanging in her living room that states: "REMEMBER THIS, when you come here, what you see here, what you hear here, when you leave here, let it stay here or don't come back here." These are powerful words that ring true. Nobody enjoys having their business or private life discussed in the public arena.

Being part of the staff team, I sometimes sit in on office meetings in which I have the opportunity to observe the group dynamics. Some people have respect for authority, as they understand that there is a manager present. Even if they have concerns, they approach them in a respectful and tactful manner. They are very constructive but not argumentative. Then there are the quiet types who hardly comment at all; however, when they do speak, they often come out with thoughtful solutions. There are also team members who are there to argue and cause disruption to the meeting. I look at all these characters, and I ask myself these questions: Which ones would I want as friends if I were to choose? To which ones would I go for advice? Which ones would I avoid? You will be surprised by the answers you come up with if you ask yourself these questions. I know most people run away from an argumentative person. The Bible says, "It is better to live in a corner of the housetop than in a house shared with a contentious wife" (Proverbs 21:9).

CHAPTER 5

Learn Discipline

Discipline requires you to control your attitude, behave yourself, and think before you speak, wherever you are.

I have had the privilege of being around managers who have positively influenced my way of thinking and the way I behave regardless of where I am. They imparted a sense of discipline to me. Maintaining a positive attitude requires discipline. Your ability to do administrative work well is not enough, as it has to go hand in hand with your attitude and how you relate and communicate with people.

Though the example I am about to set forth is in my field of work, the rationale can be applied to all work situations.

In my field of work, the service users are vulnerable adults; their needs change from time to time. For example, say a person is going about his activities of daily living with no concerns at all, but one day, one of his physical functions fails permanently and he needs support.

Please do not feel overwhelmed by the example I am going to present. Say a person has had a stroke that has left him paralyzed on the left side of his body, prevented him from swallowing food properly, and impaired his normal mobility. This means he comes under the care of my team. The team will ensure that he has a care plan tailored to the needs identified and that this plan is properly implemented. Thus, the team will provide support with the measures required to enable the client to swallow his food in line with the recommendation from a medical doctor. This will also extend to a care plan for his mobility; he may need to use a wheelchair after he has been assessed by a physiotherapist.

Because of the nature of the work, it becomes very rewarding when a staff member can pay attention to detail and immediately notice changes with a service user who may not be in a position to let the staff know. This is especially true if the person has severe learning disabilities and is unable to tell the staff what is happening to him or her. Therefore, the staff member's ability to write care plans and risk assessments for service users is vital to the health and well-being of that person.

There are some staff members who are very good at what they do. They can write very well. In my field of work, if a staff member is able to assess the changing needs of the service users, he or she can write plans and risk assessments that are useful.

Some people are able to do all the necessary paperwork, but their attitude toward their colleagues, as evidenced by the way they talk, can be perceived as difficult. Some seem domineering, while others seem to be unnecessarily challenging, which in turn makes the work difficult for other staff members.

This does not mean that they are always wrong. It should be noted, however, that too much of such conduct can intimidate other staff members who are not that dominant and confident. The attitudes described here can affect the personal development of the people who have them. These people are very good with their work, but they lack people skills.

Some people take everything said to them very personally, to such an extent that it becomes difficult for anyone to correct them or inform them that some areas of their work practices need changing. As a result, the moment a colleague talks about their shortcomings, they start crying. How do you intend to progress to the next level in your career if you cannot take constructive criticisms regarding the "needs improvement" areas of your work?

Thinking before you talk is one of the steps that you have to take toward your personal development. Some people do not think before they talk. They say anything that comes into their heads just to upset others or cause disruption in the workplace. Working with people involves using "people skills." You can attend all the training workshops in the world, including those on communication skills to do your work effectively, but simply pausing for a moment to think before you talk will alleviate you and others from all sorts of distress. It might keep you out of trouble.

There are some staff members who are very good at their jobs, but because of some of the issues mentioned in this chapter, it becomes very difficult for any manager to develop them to the next level.

Most work activities, if not all, involve people, which means that you will need "people skills." There will come a time when you will need to calm a frustrated client or satisfy a difficult one. How do you go about that? Are you tactful? Do you give the client very constructive and intelligent reasons for the "less-than-optimal" situation and apologize on behalf of your organization when you are at fault, or do you just say something out of the blue and make the situation worse?

Have you noticed that there are some staff members to whom the manager prefers to hand over the reins in his or her absence? This is because the manager knows that these staff members are capable of handling any problems that might arise. Can you count yourself as one of these staff members? Can you say that if your manager and his or her deputy or any of the senior members in the team have to be away on a training day that you will be given the responsibility to ensure that the workplace runs smoothly for that day? Or do you find yourself in the group of people who are worried and upset because you do your work very well on the shop floor, including your administrative tasks, but when it comes to your manager needing someone to take responsibility for attending to clients and other external agencies, the manager never asks you? Do you find that the manager tends to ask someone else within your rank who has the same skills you have but this person has good communication skills and a good attitude? If you are reading this book and you are asking yourself such questions, think of some of the issues discussed above. Start by asking yourself: Why does my manager always ask Mr. A. to do something I can do even though I have asked to do it? What does Mr. A. do differently that I need to learn? Such questions will challenge you to look carefully at your work practices and change some of your habits into positive ones.

Take it from me, my dear reader, there are some forms of unspoken communication that go on in every environment. Your manager will never openly admit this to you. It is your duty and responsibility to find out why one person will be considered while others will not have that same sort of attention. I understand that in life there will always be favoritism, and I am not blind to that, but more often than not, some of our own behaviors put people off, including managers. Since they have to be careful what they say as leaders of their workplaces, they will choose the person with equal skills who has a better attitude and better people skills to do the work. This is because, provided a person's behavior does not cause any disruption that would force them to take him or her through a disciplinary route, they will always ask someone who has the desired "people skills" to take responsibility.

CHAPTER 6

Communication Skills, Discipline, and Personal Responsibility

Be sensitive to unspoken communication. This will help you to be disciplined.

When at work, a "senior person" or colleague cannot tell you everything with regard to dos and don'ts. You have to learn to apply common sense to issues so you do not make the tasks of other team members difficult. Bear in mind, you are working for the clients.

For example, you know that in most workplaces, you are not supposed to use your personal mobile phone on the premises. On the other hand, your work might involve using mobile phones. If it is the nature of your job to be on the mobile phone, then that is okay. However, if you know that you are not meant to be using your personal mobile phone when attending to a client and you do it anyway, though your clients may just watch you and your colleagues may look at you but say nothing, do not be surprised when this issue comes up during your supervision. For that matter, do not be surprised if you are confronted by your manager and asked to turn your phone off, because you did not respect the code of practice and conduct of your workplace. Failing to switch your phone off during working hours shows you are not sensitive to the unspoken communication. You more or less invited the rebuke in the form of a senior member of staff asking you to switch your phone off.

At times, in order to create a calm atmosphere for people to work in, senior team members do not want to go stressing staff members on issues like the example with the phone. They expect staff members to have the decency to respect the workplace so that everyone can work in a calm and conducive environment. Therefore, one must learn not to abuse the trust that the senior team members give to all the staff. In short, most managers or senior team members will not necessarily go biting if you do not go barking unnecessarily to disturb the peace of the work environment.

Part of being sensitive to unspoken forms of communication is being sensitive to people's emotions. Though we are all human, under normal circumstances, we are not supposed to take our personal issues to work. Please learn not to do this, because no manager wants to develop someone who has all his or her personal issues being talked about at the workplace. This is because part of developing to the next level means having access to certain information that only you and your manager should know about; therefore, if you cannot keep your own personal business confidential, why would any manager want to trust you with issues of confidentiality relating to work?

However, there comes a time when you need to inform your manager about your personal issues, because you may need time off to sort these out. This means that sometimes, one way or another, our personal issues, which affect our emotions, can get in the way of our work. However, bear in mind that just as you may need to go to your manager and he may give you leeway because of personal concerns, he is also human and sometimes will not be in a good mood, which may make him blow hot or cold. You have to be sensitive to such unspoken forms of communication in order for you to work effectively at your workplace.

For example, your manager, whom you know to be the type who only makes inquiries at work when there is the need to do so and otherwise goes about his tasks without interruption, comes to work one day and begins picking on everything everyone is doing. This can be annoying if you are at the receiving end. You cannot say he is doing the wrong thing, because it is part of his duties and responsibilities, but you know him well and you know that this is not the normal way he operates. In a situation like this, you just give him room to look for the areas he wants everyone to improve on and let him know it will be done.

Straightaway, you have perceived he is not in a good mood. He did not get angry at anyone, but neither did he make the work easy for anyone that day. He did his job, but you know this is not his style. In a situation like this, you should know that now is not the time for you to go and ask him for a raise in pay, because he will look for all the faults in your work and the reasons why you do not deserve it, so wait until he is in a good mood. As the Bible puts it in Ecclesiastes 3:1, "There is a time for everything." Learn to ask things at the right time.

We are all human, and mood changes happen to all of us. If you learn to understand that managers are also humans, you will not take everything so personally and ruin the chance of your own personal development. Needless to say, I know that some managers can be very difficult to work with, but at least learn to be sensitive to their emotions, in as much as they are sensitive to yours, so that if you go to them for support during your "lows"—I mean when you are down—you will remember that they are humans and they experiences lows as well.

Discipline yourself in assertiveness to know when an opportunity presents itself and use it to your advantage.

Listen very carefully, people who want to develop themselves to the next level in their careers will be looking for what they can do to alleviate the responsibilities of the senior team members. When senior managers ask the staff team to do a task, people who want to develop volunteer to do it. Oh yes, they are doing the same work you are doing, but they have decided to take on additional responsibility because they do not want to be where they are for the rest of their lives. They go from one task to another, and soon, the manager is asking them if they want to learn more about management responsibilities. Even if your manager is not asking you to do anything during your supervision time, let him or her know that you would like to have more responsibilities, as you want to develop to the next level. *Learn to blow your trumpet for others to hear so you can get the attention you need.*

Some people want the crown without the cross, but take it from me, *the cross will always come before the crown.* If you want to develop yourself, you have to take on additional responsibilities. It is these responsibilities that will stretch your knowledge and sharpen your skills for the next level. How else will you be able to convince an interview panel that you have the necessary experience?

Being sensitive to nonverbal forms of communication involves learning positive habits.

When you are around people who are in high positions, observe what they do, their body language, the way they talk including how they speak and the words they use, and the way they carry themselves in difficult situations and learn from them. They are not perfect, but they have trained themselves by "highlighting" their positives instead of their negatives. You may think they are perfect or they cannot make mistakes, but they do. However, when they make mistakes, they learn from them and move on, and that is what you have to learn to do. Focus on your positives and reduce your negatives.

Part of being disciplined is learning to guard your tongue.

Most of us will at one point or another in our lives use the "F" word because of one situation or another. The most common expletives are "Shit!" "Oh shit," "What the fuck is that?" "Fuck!" or "Fuckin' hell!" These come out when someone has just experienced a bizarre situation, or these are the words used to justify the mistake the person has made or of letting someone know that he or she did something stupid and "If I get you, I will hang you." This may not necessarily be expressed in the words mentioned above but can also be conveyed by the way a person talks. You do not have to have a PhD in communications to communicate well with people, but polishing some of your vocabulary use is vital to your personal development. Look at it this way: how do you talk to someone you respect? You are very careful with the words you use when talking to this person, aren't you? So why not apply that to all areas of your life in which you need to communicate with others? I realized that most people in authority, when they are in public and they are upset by uncomfortable news or someone says something stupid around the table that is not worth the argument, they do not comment; the silence is enough for the person to think through what he or she said and the offender either apologizes or keeps quiet. That does not necessarily mean that such people in authority do not swear, but they have decided not to do so in public. It is as simple as that.

If you are the type who enjoys using foul language or "allowing your mouth to ride rough" by talking any way you want, thinking it is fine, you'd better watch out, because it does not enhance your reputation or give you a good one either as people consider it to be very bad verbal skills. Your superior will not be pleased with you, and he or she will be very reluctant to promote you if you are unable to discipline your own tongue. If you do not think before you talk, you could be putting off potential clients from coming to the organization. You are the big risk your manager cannot afford to take.

Discipline yourself wherever you go.

People might judge you by what you say, and based on what you say, they may want to be around you or distance themselves from you, so when you are in a social situation, learn to discipline your tongue.

A friend of mine told me about an incident that happened to her some years ago. She is a manager and decided to develop herself by doing a course in college. As a new student, she was watching everyone and looking at personalities that were favorable to her own, deciding whom she would want as her friend. As the days rolled by, people's attitudes, good or bad depending on one's perception, began to emerge. They all introduced themselves and stated what their professions were. However, this friend simply stated the work she did without mentioning the authority bit. Days passed by and she was still looking for her friend, as she told me, "Lydia, I cannot be bothered with the disrespect, so I choose my friends; they do not choose me." I think there is wisdom in that. Anyway, soon, she found someone who, like her, did not enjoy arguments, and she was thrilled. As the course progressed, she heard one of her fellow black colleagues giving an example in class of how he would not want to work under a black manager because black managers always have to please the "higher up" and, therefore, staff working under them suffer. My friend, being black and a manager, told me she was so furious she felt like jumping out of her chair and punching him in the mouth, but she kept her cool. So guess what happened when, in the course of time, he got to know that my friend was a manager. He forgot what he had said and even had the effrontery to come and ask my friend for a job. You see, he was damned by his tongue. How on earth can anyone who has demonstrated such behavior expect to be offered a job?

It pays to discipline yourself wherever you go, because you never know to whom you are talking. This person could be your next bridge to your breakthrough or the lifeline to your deadline, and it all depends on your attitude.

As long as we are on Planet Earth, we will depend on one another; we are all interdependent.

Discipline your tongue wherever you are, because what you say can have an effect on people closer to you in an unknown environment, and they can stretch their hand to help you or they can become very wary of you because of your tongue. In short, learn not to talk just any way anywhere.

In addition, one thing people forget is that no one wants to work with someone who is contentious. Managers also owe it to themselves to maintain good cordial relationships with their higher-ups. Most managers are too intelligent to risk such relationships. The person in the real-life story did not see it that way, however; he saw it as a weakness, but after discovering who my friend was, then he was trying to be nice and pleasing to this same person to get a post in her team. And this was after complaining that most black managers always want to please their higher-ups. Talk about the kettle calling the pot black. This story tells us that we cannot live like an island or a lone ranger. We need people to help us to develop to the next level in our career path. We can meet them anywhere, and we will not even know that such a person is in our midst. Only when we have demonstrated negative behaviors and then want those people to welcome us in to their fold, which they will vehemently refuse to do, will we know.

Being disciplined makes you well grounded in all areas of your life.

Competence goes hand in hand with discipline.

If you are competent in doing something, you need to have the discipline to maintain it and to develop it to the next level for your career development. In fact, the most difficult achievements in life require discipline, not only in achieving the purpose but also in maintaining it.

General Mistakes that People Make

Let us talk about the generalities of things that go on in our lives. Do you know that there are some routines in our lives that promote self-discipline? All of us have routines—for example, the daily routines of showering before work, eating and drinking, sleeping, and going to church or the mosque on a regular basis. These are all routines; however, there are some particular routines that enhance our competence and promote good self-discipline toward our career development. For example, getting to work on time—you can be competent with your work, but if you have a history of being late, your colleagues who are waiting for you to come to work on time so they can go home will not be pleased with you and neither will your manager. Despite the fact that you are good with your work, your lateness is causing unhappiness in the workplace. You will therefore need to be disciplined to address this and be able to arrive at work on time.

Having Respect for Authority

It takes discipline to have respect for others in general. If you have no respect for anyone, you will not respect the one who is in authority over you. I have seen people unable to hold down a job because they are disrespectful, so that one way or another, the manager has to find a way of failing them in their probation.

Having respect for authority does not mean you are afraid of your manager or are passive and allow anything to be done to you. It means you are able to understand that there is a leader there to ensure that tasks are done; otherwise, the work will not go on, and if tasks are not done, people will not be paid, and soon there will be redundancies. How do you intend to earn respect if you are not ready to give it? Who will want to develop or promote a disrespectful person? No one.

Doing What Is Expected of You

Do your work diligently within the allocated time. If for any reason you are unable to complete your task, let the next person taking over from you know why. Do not deliberately leave tasks undone, expecting the next person on duty to take up your responsibility, because he or she will soon go to the manager with complaints, and when this person does, please do not say that he or she is picking on you. Some will even go to the extent of praying to God in church for other colleagues at the workplace to stop giving them hell, but if they will sit down and be honest with themselves, they will realize that they are their own nemesis. Managers know all their staff, and they know the hard workers and those who will not cause any harm but will not put in too much more effort than their normal work. They will promote according to your strengths, so if you want career development, then do what is expected of you.

Time Management at Work

Part of being disciplined is managing your time wisely in your area of competence. For example, if you have a workload, prioritize the most important tasks for the day to be done first and in that order, one after the other to the least important one. Ensure that you give all your work time limits so that you become conscious of your time and are able to do most or all the tasks for the day. If some of your tasks were not done because of the time factor, put them in the diary for the next day.

Disciplining yourself to manage your time wisely will also include not answering phone calls when you are doing tasks. You will be amazed at the time that you can spend talking on the phone and how much could have been done if you compare the time spent talking to the time allocated for each task.

Focus and Organize Your Tasks

When doing tasks, focus on them and learn to complete one task before jumping to another one. First and foremost, you have to know what you want to do. Then you must plan what you want to do. Organize every task you are about to do, prioritize them in order, write them on paper, and number them according to their priority of importance, and then give them time limits for completion. For example, assuming you are on duty at work today from 9:00 AM to 5:00 PM and the tasks below are your tasks in the diary for the day, you can prioritize them as follows:

Task 1: Check diary for business commitments of the day = 10 mins.
Task 2: Answer e-mail = 20 mins.
Task 3: Make important phone calls = 20 mins.
Task 4: Write a proposal for a business meeting = 2½ hrs.
Task 5: Lunch break = 30 mins.
Task 6: Staff meeting at 1:00 PM (Expected Duration) = 2 hrs.
Task 7: Meeting with Mr. Thompson at 3.30 PM (Expected Duration) =1 hr. 20 mins.

Closing time: 5:00 PM

Be realistic with the time needed for each task and get a clock or watch to check the time as you do your tasks so that you do not fall behind. Be sure that you complete task 1 before you go to task 2. When you organize your tasks, focus solely on them without any external disruptions whatsoever. When you allocate time for each task, you will realize that you will have enough time to get your workload done and even be able to do other tasks that a senior person might ask you to do.

Delegate

Though you are competent with your work, learn to delegate tasks to other staff members you think are capable of doing them. You can ask them if they want to do the task. Just because you do not like doing a particular task does not necessary mean that they would not like it. Always remember that what you hate another may love. You might not enjoy working with numbers, but another member of your team might enjoy numbers a lot, so if you have anything that involves accounting and they are good at it, why don't you let them look at that type of paperwork? Never assume that you are the only one who can do everything well, because there is the off chance that some team members could do it much better if they were given the chance. Delegate but only with tasks that are not sensitive or for your eyes only as a senior person.

As a senior carer, when my manager delegated tasks to me, I looked at the ones that the carers were capable of doing and delegated those tasks to them. This gave me the room to concentrate on the ones that only I could do, and it also saved me time, because I was able to do other things as well. Therefore, by the time my manager required the results of the tasks she had given me, I had done more than she had asked me to do and I did not do it all by myself. I asked the carers I was overseeing to do the ones they were capable of doing. Even when they were working on the "shop floor," I looked at their abilities and strengths and delegated what I knew some of them did better than I, and they did it much better than I would have. This does not make me incompetent in my work; rather, I have identified the "not-so-strong" areas in my work and I have realized that some staff members are much better at these tasks than I am. Why should I deny them what they do best?

You've got to have the humility to recognize that others will do some things much better than you. Do not be jealous of them; rather, acknowledge their gifts and utilize them to your advantage.

Self-Control

You can be competent in what you do, but if you do not have discipline and self-control, you stand at risk of losing everything you have worked hard for.

For example, let's say you are an accountant and you have been entrusted with the finances of your organization. If you take any amount from the coffers for personal use, this amounts to financial abuse and an abuse of trust. So when the money in the bank and what is on paper do not add up, you end up losing your job. Though you are competent in your job, your lack of self-discipline to control your hand has caught up with you, and you have lost your job as a result.

Temper

Some people just have a temper the size of the earth. They get agitated at everything. Part of being able to work with people is learning to control your temper. That is a big part of having people skills. Though not often, there are times you might come across very difficult or verbally abusive clients who are angry about particular aspects of a service given to them, and, for this reason, they are being verbally challenging. It is your duty and responsibility to calm them down, inasmuch as their behavior is not allowed at your workplace; however, the services you provide them have made them agitated, so how do you intend to calm such persons down when you are triggered by the smallest of any nonsense said to you? That does not mean that you have to endure being verbally abused—no, that is not what I am saying. Hear me out. What I am trying to point out is that there will be extreme cases in which you are going to meet some not-very-nice people. When those times come, how will you handle the situation if you are short-tempered yourself?

CHAPTER 7

Mentors

Who Are Mentors?

Mentors are people who have knowledge in a particular domain or specialist expertise that you are interested in pursuing. These are people with whom you might like to consult in your development to the next level. They are like a bridge that connects you to the next dimension of your life.

You will need mentors at every stage of your life, and you will have different types of mentors. You will be closer to some than to others.

Mentors are teachers; they need not necessarily be in the classroom. They are teachers of well-experienced life skills who impart such knowledge to you.

For example, the spiritual person or pastor of your church who you look up to with so much respect is your spiritual mentor, because you consult him or her often in times of difficulty, during which you may consider the need for divine intervention. You ask this person to help you in prayers.

You can also have an attorney as a mentor. This is the person whom you consult when you require explanations of certain aspects of the law. Though this person is not necessarily your friend, you have the privilege to consult with him or her, while others cannot.

The mentor closest to you is your main mentor, the one whom you sometimes feel like kicking because he or she does not agree with everything you say and will be the first to point out your mistakes.

Mentors will want to see you develop to the next phase of your career.

They know what you do not know.

Mentors save you from making a lot of mistakes, as they have been there and can share their acquired knowledge and experiences with you. The years of mistakes they have learned from and the subsequent problems they have rectified will save you a lifetime of setbacks.

They are able to introduce you to prominent people in your career pathway who can change your life for the better.

They will link you to others who will help you to succeed if they are not in a position to do so.

Mentors are selfless toward their protégés.

Mentors are not afraid you will not like what they say; in fact, they expect you to heed their fair warning rather than sing your praises.

They, however, do give you praise when it is due.

They will let you know when you are deviating from your purpose or goals, because they will not want to see you let your ambition or destiny go down the drain. They are the ones who will give you the honest and straight talk.

Mentors do not expect you to like them, but they expect you to respect them. You need to do so, as they, in all honesty, point out where your shortfalls are. You often might not like their comments, but you will always thank them for pointing out to you potential problems when you realize the damage those problems might have inflicted on you had you not listened to them.

Mentors may not necessarily be your friends, though some of your friends can be your mentors. Maybe you have just not noticed it.

Remember, mentors are human, and they are by no means perfect. They can and will make mistakes too, but do not let that jeopardize a good relationship. Focus most often on their positives rather than their negatives.

Why Is It Important to Have a Mentor?

It is important because there will always be someone in your field of work who knows something you do not.

You will need advice on decisions you will have to make at different points in your life; therefore, there is nothing like having people who have been through these situations. They are able to tell you what to do and what not to do.

If you want to be a great leader, you have to learn to acquire the knowledge of great minds.

It is good for your career development.

The guidance of a mentor can save you from trouble.

Mentors are very important, because the days of the lone ranger are long gone. You stand alone, and falling is very easy, but when you have a rock behind you in the form of a mentor, when the need arises, he or she can introduce you to others who will come to your aid and help you out of your crisis.

Mentors are the lifeline to your professional deadline.

Mentors are teachers who open doors to the next level in your career development. Needless to say, I got my first position in management because I learned from a mentor who alerted those at the higher levels that I had talent. But for her, it would have taken years for my talents to be discovered. One person changed my life by cutting back years just by introducing me to people who matter.

In life, all you need is the right key to the right door, and mentors are the keys who will unlock the right doors.

Some of your friends are your mentors; you have just not taken notice of it.

Do you categorize your friends into groups? If you do not, then I suggest you start doing it today. You will realize that some of them have been mentoring you along the way.

I have some friends with whom I do not chat casually. They like to know the wisdom of the conversation. This does not mean that they do not have any sense of humor; rather, they are, by their natural temperaments, telling me, "I am a serious person, and whatever you have to say has got to be worth talking about; otherwise, do not talk about it." In short, if you have nothing concrete to say, then don't speak. I realized along the way though that these people will be the first to comfort me when situations go badly for me. They are not necessarily always present around me, but they will turn up at my door if the situation demands it. Most of the time though, they will spend hours with me on the phone, at the expense of their phone bill if necessary, to let me know that they are just a phone call away and that they are thinking of me. They are also the first to tell me, "That was very badly done, Lydia," and they are the very people who would also say, "I am very proud of you."

Among my friends, there are a few such people. I sometimes get angry at what they say, but they still tell me. They say, "I know that you are upset, but I have told you anyway. The most important thing is that you have heard what I have said. Think carefully before you make that decision."

Writing this book has made me realize what a blessing they are to me. I always contact them because even though I get agitated with their honesty, I know that they will call a spade a spade, call it as they see it, and do so without mincing words. Their views on a matter enable me to see how others will perceive a particular situation.

When I must make a decision in which logic and reasoning are important, there are some friends I will never consult, because I know that even my stupidest decisions are fine with them. I mean that everything I do, they will back me 100 percent. Now, that does not make them bad friends; they just like me good or bad. But you see, anytime I am down and I need someone to cheer me up, I can always count on these friends of mine. I can be assured of getting better soon. This is something I will never get from the first group of friends I described earlier. I therefore need all of them in my life for specific reasons. In fact, they are also a blessing because not everyone can make you feel better. These friends always see the light at the end of the tunnel no matter how dark it is.

It is for this reason that you will need to determine the nature of your friends, assess them, and know who you can count on in a crisis, whom to go to when you are down and need cheering up, and whom to go to when you need advice.

Your manager can be your mentor.

If you are closer to your manager or a "senior person" who shows you how to do more than your job description requires, then such a person is your mentor. This person is indirectly training you for the next level and most often is the one to inform you that a post is coming up. He or she may say, "I think with all the work that you have been doing, you are capable of doing that job, so apply for the post."

Your mentors will come in different ages, genders, and sexual orientations.

Your mentors should not necessarily be mature or older people. Some will be younger than you. They may be male or female. They may come from a different race, culture, or religion. They may be of another sexual orientation. They may display many facets of the human race, so you have to rise above your stereotyping, prejudicial thinking, and personal beliefs and look at their talents, abilities, experiences, and skills instead, if you want to acquire their knowledge. If you go to them with your "judgmental eye," you will not receive the knowledge you require, because they will see through you and will not open up to you.

For example, most men in general will not admit it, but they do not want their manager to be a woman. They often feel a bit like they are not being the strong "macho guy" because a woman is telling them what to do. However, if a man has a woman as his manager and sees her as a competent person whom God created in the form of the opposite gender, there will be a good working relationship between them, and the man will in turn learn a lot from the female manager about what it takes to become a manager.

Some older people have issues when the manager is younger than they are. If the manager is the same age as their child or grandchildren, why should they listen to him or her? For the older person, it is meant to be the other way round. Listen, if age was the measurement for work competences, abilities, skills, talents, experience, and wisdom, then all the elderly would be in the posts and the young adults would have no work to do. It is therefore not about how old you are, but how competent you are. However, some staff members who are older than their managers cannot humble themselves a little bit for their own personal development to acquire the knowledge that this young person has.

As far as they are concerned, they are older, so they know more than the young managers. If you were that competent, why did the organization not look at your age and put you there as manager? They are so blinded with anger that a young person is their manager they never see the talent, and in so doing, they lose a potential mentor right under their very noses.

In my next book, which consists of inspirational poems, I have a poem that describes mentors coming from all walks of life and the opportunity that people miss simply because they did not look at the talents of others but rather at their own prejudices and stereotypes. The poem is called "Catch the Anointing in the Prophet."

Catch the Anointing in the Prophet

There are some dimensions in my life where my talent will take me
where my background becomes invalid.
The fact that I come from an unfavorable background does not mean
that my back is on the ground.
My talents will take me beyond the shores of my wildest dreams.
Breaking boundaries and territories from my humble beginnings.
I will therefore hone my talents to perform to the best of my abilities.
You cannot define me by my race, age, religion, culture, gender,
sexual orientation, or disability because you will be looking for the talent
within me and not my physical being.
Some will miss their blessing because I came in the form of a woman or man.
Some will miss their blessing because I came in the form of a white person, black, Asian, and all that
variety the beauty of the Infinite Intelligence created in his own wisdom.
If you would look beyond your prejudices and stereotyping, you will not
miss the opportunity through my talent.
You will see the vision in the visionary.
The Infinite Intelligence puts his treasures in vessels of different
origins and races.
God is not going to apologize to any human being because he chose me.
Like the sages of old, I come to you with my talent to be part of the
problem-solving gurus of the human race in my generation.
Like John the Baptist in the Bible, I will say catch the anointing
in the prophet irrespective of how he looks because if you look at the
physical image of John the Baptist you will miss the anointing.
Some talents are hidden within people we consider as unworthy by
our own self-made standards.
But if we break down the barriers and see what is within them
and not what is without, we will see the shining star within.
Their talents will be beneficial and a blessing unto us.
I may come from an unfavorable background but my back is not on the ground.

How Do You Get Mentors?

Most of what we have discussed has shown you how you can get some of your mentors. These are work colleagues or superiors, friends, and fellow church members; however, if you want to set up your own business and you need a mentor who has done extraordinarily well in that field, you need to go beyond your manager. These are some of the questions to ask that can help you in taking the necessary steps to find your mentor.

- Have you started your own business? If so, do you need advice or have questions to ask?
- In whose footsteps do you want to follow?
- Are they the best in your chosen field?
- Do you know these mentors' workplaces?
- Have you thought of calling them, or have you tried? If not, why not?
- Does your mentor hold seminars, or do other great minds hold seminars in fields similar to yours at which you can acquire knowledge to the benefit of your business?
- Do you attend these seminars? If not, why not?

As a writer, I read a lot. I read, read, and read. I like reading because I like to broaden my knowledge. I believe that most of the things I do not know are hidden in a book somewhere. I just have to find that book, like I have to find mentors to learn and acquire that knowledge to my advantage. Most of my mentors are spiritual leaders, because my gift is writing solely on inspiration. A word they say just triggers that divine intelligence, so I always want to be around such people who trigger my talent; therefore, anytime I know that one of my mentors is coming to the United Kingdom, I will take time off work and be there to acquire his or her knowledge. It is not necessarily the biblical preaching that I listen to, but particular concepts, sentences, and words that will trigger my inspiration. To this end, I find myself writing poems. A few of my friends who have had the opportunity to listen to my poems liken them to the Psalms. They also claim that the poems give them a sense of calm and produce a peaceful effect. I call these poems "angelic writings." This book, however, is not that type of writing, but my next books will reflect such themes.

Read and watch autobiographies and biographies of your mentors.

Reading autobiographies of your mentors gives you a lot of information about the challenges they faced on their pathway to success, how they dealt with issues when they arose and how they succeeded. Watch programs that feature your mentors and television channels that show biographies of great personalities, both living and dead, as this will broaden your knowledge and understanding about how such people lived their lives and what made them so distinct from others.

One of the things that people will not want to do is call a prominent person who has done so well in business. They say, "Why would he want to talk to me? He might be too busy. Why would he be interested in my mushroom business?" Oh yes, I know it will take a while for you to get through to a well-established businessperson but persistent calls to his or her personal assistant will let that person know that you really need his or her knowledge. You will be amazed to learn that most mentors are ready to impart their knowledge to people who are willing just to ask. As Matthew 7:7 puts it, "Ask and it shall be given unto you." It is rare for a mentor to say no to you; however, if you do get in touch with one who says no, just find another one; that is why God gave a lot of people talents in the same field. Find someone else if one person shuts the door in your face. Never feel down or be put off by it. Take it as part of life. In life's journey, some will say yes and some will say no. The only thing they can say is no and nothing else, so do not be afraid to call your mentor, as it will open doors of lifetime opportunities for you.

CHAPTER 8

Identify Your Talent

We all have different talents, skills, and abilities. It is our duty and responsibility to find out what we are good at; how we can develop these talents, skills, and abilities to our advantage; and how we can earn a living out of it.

Ask yourself these questions:

- What am I good at?
- What is it that I do effortlessly? What comes so naturally to me it is like a hobby, and yet I can earn money from?
- What do I do for others for free and they always come for more?
- Have you asked them why they like what you do?

If you have discovered your talent and you are unsure about it, do you know of any people who are doing something similar? If you do, you can contact them and learn their systems, but you should always maintain the originality of your talent. There should always be a clear difference between your work and that of others, so learn to maintain and make a clear distinction in your originality in your area of expertise. Just as Elisha the prophet told the widow to go and borrow vessels for him to fill with her own oil (2 Kings 4:1–6), so must you treat your talent. Borrow systems that people use to develop their businesses, but your talent must be unique. It is your own oil; you just borrow the vessels, which are the systems they used to develop their business.

The fact that no one is doing what you are doing does not necessarily mean that your talent is not a good one. Some people have extraordinary talents that no one has had before. New discoveries occur all the time, so you need to hold on to your dreams, believe in them, and look for those who can finance them.

I discovered that my inspirational writings or "angelic writings" lift people's moods when I started writing just for fun on my Facebook page. I discovered that a lot of people became interested and looked forward to reading my messages as they would write very encouraging words and say how much they liked them. I was amazed. One time, I was piled up with college assignments, so I did not write those inspirational messages for two days. I was overwhelmed with e-mails asking whether I was ill or if something serious had happened to me. It was then that I discovered that I had a talent I had not tapped into.

What Do You Do When You Identify Your Talent?

Some of the topics to be discussed in this section will guide you on what to do when you identify your talent.

Study.

When you identify your talent and life skills, develop them by broadening your knowledge, by studying in that field so you can be the best in that area of expertise. For example, if you are good with accounting, computers, and mathematics, find courses relating to such disciplines and enroll in them. There are some fields that might require you to have a university degree to be the best in your chosen area. Do not be afraid of the amount of academic work that comes with your dream; go and do the course. Remember that most of the good things in life take time to achieve; they do not come easily. So you need to sacrifice some years and effort to be able to achieve the level of success you want.

In life, everything changes; nothing stays the same, so therefore, if you do not study in your chosen field, you will soon be out-of-date with the current information relating to your work. Always remember, people will go to the person who is currently solving the challenges of today to find solutions to their problems, not the one who is mentally out-of-date and therefore unable to produce positive results or is producing outdated results that do not solve current issues.

Read books and journals relating to your talent.

Read books and journals relating to your talent or your chosen field. This not only broadens your knowledge but exposes you to current issues, which could be modern developments or current government legislation affecting your chosen field.

Go borrow vessels by acquiring other people's knowledge.

As a writer, I read a lot, because I have to if I want to be a good writer. I follow in the footsteps of my mentors, but I also maintain my talent.

I gave an example from the Bible in which the prophet Elisha asked the widow to go and borrow vessels so that he could fill them with her own oil. This means that you have to "go borrow vessels" by reading, observing the current systems, doing what others in your chosen field are doing, or using what they are using to develop and maximize their talent or business to broaden your knowledge for use in your area of expertise.

I asked you to "borrow systems" others have implemented and are using, not copy them; you have to maintain the originality of your talent. You do your work in such a way that the moment anyone sees it they definitely know it is you. That is what I am talking about. Do not go doing exactly the same thing that another company or organization is doing; otherwise, you will soon end up in court for copying other people's ideas. Learn what makes them successful and then mix it with what you have or are doing, but keep your talent untainted.

In management, this is called benchmarking. I can look at a document pertaining to procedures or policies someone has implemented at their workplace, which are working very well, and if I realize they will be good for my workplace, I will look at the areas in which they will be suitable and use some of the good practices the person implemented—not necessarily what he or she has written but the wisdom behind it.

For example, as someone writing a book for the first time, I read and look at the style of people who write the kind of books I want to write, how they gather their thoughts and how they present them on paper. What I do not do is copy their ideas. If I have to quote writers, I give them their due by citing the source of that quotation.

Update yourself.

Everything in life changes, except inanimate objects. You therefore have to ensure that you go to training and workshops to enable you to be on top of your game.

Your Jar of Oil

Your talent is your jar of oil. When the prophet Elisha spoke to the widow in 2 Kings 4:2, he asked her a question: "What do you have in the house?"

She responded by saying, "I have nothing but a jar of oil."

You have your talent, but you have to be able to make it more useful or "user friendly" for others to benefit from it if you want to generate wealth.

For example, I have a friend who is very good with computers. He repaired them and did all kinds of work relating to computers for various companies. He realized that there is a market for training others, so he developed his own workshops in which he imparts his knowledge to others. In so doing, he turned his talent into a business. He looked beyond working for other companies and created a business of his own because he saw a need.

My question to you, dear reader, is: have you identified a need in your chosen field? And if you have identified a need, what are you doing about it? Have you thought of taking steps to meet those needs? That is how your mind has to work if you intend to generate wealth and be a success.

Have you thought of doing workshops and training others? If, in your chosen field, there is no one training or doing workshops, you are successful at what you do, and others are in that sort of business, don't you think that there will be the need for workshops and training in that field?

If you intend to start a workshop, you might need to look at how people who do workshops go about it, which means that you might have to allocate time to go to workshops to learn how they are done and also ask questions of the one providing the workshop about what is involved in organizing a successful workshop. How much will it cost? Some places for workshops are quite a bit cheaper than others. What does putting on workshops entail? Maybe you'll need to borrow a projector for your PowerPoint presentation. How do you advertise your workshop? Will it be through the media, the Internet, or billboards? Whom do you need to contact to make this happen? Who is your target audience, and how can you reach them? If you have not thought about it, then this is food for thought for you.

Read government legislation and policies governing your talent or chosen field.

Government legislations affect businesses; in fact, they affect all citizens in a country, so you have to be conversant with current government legislations relating to your business so that you are able to project your turnover and profits in the coming years. Remember, nothing stays the same; therefore, your talent, which you have turned into a business, has to be able to move with the times and be able to outlive you.

For example, if a government legislation requires that for you to continue operating in your business you need to register with a new government body and that for anyone to be a member of staff in your business, he or she needs to have a certain amount of qualifications or "checks" done on them with a recognized body, you have to abide by those regulations if you want your business to continue and flourish.

Know what your clients need, and then modernize your talent and find out what you can do to meet those needs.

You have to be able to reach your customers to find out what they need. Ask questions when they purchase your product. You can do a questionnaire survey that asks what they think of your product, if they have any comments as to how to make it much better, or if there are any areas at all with which they are pleased or displeased. If they are pleased, ask why, and if not, ask why not. Ask them for only two minutes of their time to fill in this questionnaire.

If you have a website, you need to have a comment section to enable others to leave comments as to what they think of your product or the service you are offering them. You have to look at these comments and take them in good faith to develop your business. Remember, not all the comments will be nice, but you should still take what is being said even if you do not agree with it and build something good out of it.

I acquire the most wisdom for free from people not when they are pleased with me but when they are agitated and angry because of something I did or did not do. You will be amazed as to the intelligence and wisdom you will find coming from people when they are upset; some of their thoughts can be very revealing indeed. Accept what they say, good or bad, and use it to improve on your talents.

Most telephone companies do this regularly. They do not always call you to ask about your views with regard to their services, but in the middle of your call to them, they will ask if you could spare only two minutes to answer questions as to how you see their service to you. Sometimes when they finish talking to you, they immediately ask you how you saw their service that day. People will let them know where they did well and where they need to improve.

I have a friend who sells me beauty products; she has analyzed how long it will take me to use up the products depending on how much I order, and the moment I am nearly out, she will text me, reminding me that I need to reorder my products. She does not wait for me to call her and say I am about to run out of some products. She does it automatically, and at times, she introduces me to new products. That is a business mind. She is good in sales, and for this reason, she has so many clients. She is always going from one place to another doing makeup for people, snapping pictures for them to see how they look and what the current products can do for their skin, asking clients to use samples of the product and what they think of it, and inviting them to attend her workshops. That is how you have to enlarge your talent to generate wealth.

CHAPTER 9

Have a Passion for Your Career

Do not start a career or course of study in a field for which you have no passion.

More often than not, it will lead to failure or you will be miserable. Can you imagine getting up on a daily basis to go to a job you hate for the rest of your life? How awful would that be? Do not follow the crowd by doing what everyone else is doing; do what you do best. Put your talent first. The only time you should follow the crowd is when you want to "borrow their systems" and borrow what is applicable to your talent.

For example, if you are not too keen on mathematics, do not force yourself to become a mathematician. It just will make you frustrated, and you will not enjoy doing it. If you are very good in sales, you have to join the sales department and learn more about it.

My nephew has a master's degree in information systems, a field he enjoys a lot. He has a passion for numbers and computers. He once told me about an interesting experience. I will never forget it or the wise decision he made that time. In secondary school, he was very good with mathematics, and he had a friend who was very good in the arts. They were about to enter their fourth year. This is the time when tutors advise students on the sort of courses they need to choose for their pathway to the final year. Tutors also teach the students in all the courses; the students are to figure out within a two-week period which ones they resonate with to enable them to make the best possible choice for their course.

He saw some of his mates choose a science class. Some of the other students who were not taking the science class were full of accolades for those who were taking it. He was carried away by this, so he and his friend joined the science class. But because they did not understand science, he and his friend decided to change out of the science course. He said staying in that science class would have been the biggest mistake of his life, as his colleagues who did not understand the science curriculum and went on sitting in that class to show off all failed when they sat for the "ordinary levels," while he had distinction and his friend had grade 1. They pursued their courses to the university. Today, both of them are working in very reputable firms, and they are doing very well with their careers. All this happened because wisdom came to the rescue.

> "Wisdom is the principal thing; therefore get wisdom; and with all thy getting get understanding."
> —Proverbs 4:7

You do have a choice.

You have a choice to develop your talent and make it a reality.

For example, I enjoy working with disabled adults. I love every bit of it. I love to make a difference in the life of someone who cannot communicate verbally and needs support to lead a fulfilling life. Seeing these disabled adults responding to me with nonverbal communication is a great joy to me;

that is my passion, but I know there are some people who might be miserable in the same job. Are they bad people? Absolutely not. That kind of work just isn't their passion.

Most people never discover their talents. Be thankful and do something about yours.

Most people never discover their talents, not because they do not want to, but because they never pursue it. Some people's talents are obvious; they are very good at certain things from an early age. Everyone knows what they will be, and they pursue that course to be the best in that chosen field; others discover their talents by accident. I am one of the latter. I have explained how I discovered that I can write inspirational messages to life people's mood. I was just doing it for fun, but people's reactions to it made me see it in an entirely different light. However, I am working, and without my work, I would not have been able to get the financial means to get my book published. I had an idea, but I needed to "borrow" a publisher's "vessel," which cost money.

My point is it is all right to go to work, but do not sit on your talent. More often than not, it is your talent that generates the kind of wealth your daily work cannot.

That is why you have to know what you feel so passionate about, and then you can pursue it. If you have a job you are doing, that is good, as you might need to save some money from it to start a business in what you are passionate about. Please, my dear reader, do not go to the grave with your talent. Use it to contribute to humanity.

CHAPTER 10

Handling Rejection

How do you handle rejection? Do you know that rejection can be a blessing if you do not let it destroy you? We will all face rejection of some sort as long as we are on Planet Earth. However, how we handle it is what makes the difference. There is always going to be someone who does not like you or does not agree with your views and opinions. I have never known of anyone who has no enemies. If everyone likes you, there is something wrong with you. All successful people have faced rejection at some point in their lives. They have experienced the pain, the failures, and the disappointments. Why do they go on to succeed? They stick with it! They get knocked down and get back up again. The difference between successful people and nonachievers is that successful people never let these rejections destroy them or get in the way of their dreams. They learn from failures, dust themselves off, and move on.

Have you heard of J. K. Rowling? The creator of Harry Potter was rejected over and over again by various publishers until a tiny publishing company by the name of Bloomsbury published her book. Ms. Rowling reportedly earned $400 million for her first three Harry Potter books, which have been printed in thirty-five languages and sold over thirty million copies. Her fourth book in the popular series entitled *Harry Potter and the Goblet of Fire* pre-sold over one million advanced copies with a first printing of fifty-three million, which propelled her to the *New York Times* bestseller list. Can you imagine the wealth of talent that could have been buried forever if she had accepted rejection when most publishers refused to publish her book?

J. K. Rowling believed in her dream. What a lesson for us all! Learn to focus on your dream in the face of rejection. Again, rejection will come at some point in our lives; the way we handle it is what makes the difference. It is true that one man's trash is another man's treasure. You must keep trying after you face rejection.

CHAPTER 11

It's All in Your Head!

In life, none of us is exempt from challenges. It is the way we perceive these challenges that makes all the difference.

One does not drown by falling in the well; one drowns by staying there. If you think in your heart that you will overcome the obstacles in your life, you will overcome them. You can learn to confront your pain, your fears, and whatever troubling situations you find yourself in.

You can learn to grapple with adversity and move on with your life.

Great Personalities Who Showed Courage in the Face of Adversity

We all like to hear the awesome stories of courageous people, but we too often forget that courageous people are human beings just like us. What makes them so remarkable is that they decided to leave their comfort zone and pay a high price to be where they are. Abraham Lincoln is an example of what you can do if you believe in yourself and your dream. He endured thirty years of failure before he was elected president. Below are his successes and failures.

- 1831—Lost his job at age twenty-two
- 1832—Defeated in his run for Illinois state legislature at age twenty-three
- 1833—Failed in business at age twenty-five
- 1834—Elected to Illinois State Legislature at age twenty-five
- 1835—Sweetheart died when he was twenty-six
- 1836—Had a nervous breakdown at age twenty-seven
- 1838—Defeated in run for Illinois House speaker at age twenty-nine
- 1843—Defeated in run for nomination for U.S. Congress at age thirty-four
- 1846—Elected to Congress at age thirty-seven
- 1848—Lost reelection at age thirty-nine
- 1849—Rejected for land officer position at age forty
- 1854—Defeated in run for U.S. Senate forty-five
- 1856—Defeated in run for nomination for vice president at age forty-seven
- 1858—Again defeated in run for U.S. Senate at age forty-nine
- 1860—Elected president at age fifty-one

Finally, after thirty years of failure, he won the presidential election. Abraham Lincoln believed in tenacity. "My great concern," wrote our sixteenth president, "is not whether you have failed, but whether you are content with your failure."

Another inspiring personality is Chad Varah, the founder of The Samaritans. Varah was a vicar with a lot of responsibilities in his day. He was the vicar of St. Paul's in Clapham Junction, chaplain of St. John's Hospital Battersea, a staff scriptwriter and a visualizer for the *Eagle and Girl* comics. He was busy minding his own business until he had an emergency phone call that changed his life forever, and he changed the world in his lifetime because he believed he could. He founded The Samaritans in London in 1953 at the age of twenty-five. The Samaritans is a charitable organization that supports suicidal people and keeps them from committing suicide. His legacy still lives on after his death. In his own words, he states,

> It had been 18 years since I made my debut in the ministry by burying a 14 year old girl who'd killed herself when her periods started, thinking it was VD. I'd done nothing about suicide, but got myself labelled a dirty old man at 25 by seizing every opportunity to teach young people about sex, and finding that it led youngsters to join my youth clubs and young couples to come for marriage preparation, and couples drifting apart to seek marriage guidance before it was invented.

In the 1950s, suicide was a felony, and the Samaritans' psychiatrists were among those who worked to change the law. He continues,

> Then I read in some digest that there were three suicides a day in Greater London. What were they supposed to do if they didn't want a Doctor or Social Worker from our splendid Welfare State? What sort of a someone might they want? Well, some had chosen me, because of my liberal views. If it was so easy to save lives, why didn't I do it all the time? How, I answered myself, and live on what? And how would they get in touch at the moment of crisis? (The Samaritans' Web site)

The Samaritans' Web site tells us what he went on to do:

> In 1974 Chad founded Befrienders International (now Befrienders Worldwide), the worldwide body of Samaritans branches, to complement the, by then, 160 Branches in the UK and Ireland, with 18,022 volunteers. There has been a steady growth since that date, with volunteer numbers peaking in 1993 at 23,500. Calls to Samaritans have continued to go up every year, and the number of branches is now at 202. (The Samaritans Website)[2]

Look at what one man did in his lifetime? He saw a need, and he responded to it. He was even called a dirty old man for trying to save lives, but he never gave up. He challenged the status quo of the conventional way of doing things and founded an organization that is saving lives to this day.

What if Chad had given up or said he had a lot of work to do because he was a very busy man? What if he had listened to all the ridicule? I believe suicide rates would have been enormous at the time and much more so today and The Samaritans would not have been founded. He gave it his all, his best, because he believed he could.

Chad Varah is an example of how you have to pursue your dreams irrespective of the adversities you face along the way. There will always be critics. Those who can't achieve anything themselves have all the time in the world to criticize others. Of course, the moment you succeed, all their criticism stops and they start praising you.

Successful people are hardworking and deserve all that they have achieved, because if success were easily achievable, everyone would be successful. They paid the price for it, and they have every right to enjoy the rewards of their hard work in every single way.

---

2   www.samaritans.org.

CHAPTER 12

Have Faith!

Doctors at times find it difficult to explain why two people with the same illness, taking the same medication get different results. One has beaten the illness and lived, while the other just gave up and died. The difference is *attitude*. This shows how powerful our thinking is. Positive people are happy people, not because they do not face challenges in life, but because they have learned to bounce back and are even thankful in the midst of adversity.

Develop a "can-do" spirit, because "can-do" people are achievers, and they become successful people. The poem below expresses that.

It Couldn't Be Done

Somebody said that it couldn't be done,
But he with a chuckle replied
That "maybe it couldn't," but he would be one
Who wouldn't say so till he'd tried.
So he buckled right in with the trace of a grin
On his face. If he worried he hid it.
He started to sing as he tackled the thing
That couldn't be done, and he did it.
Somebody scoffed: "Oh you'll never do that;
At least no one ever has done it";
But he took off his coat and he took off his hat,
And the first thing we knew he'd begun it.
With a lift of his chin and a bit of a grin,
If any doubt rose he forbid it.
He started to sing as he tackled the thing
That couldn't be done, and he did it.
There are thousands to tell you it cannot be done,
There are thousands to prophesy failure;
There are thousands to point out to you, one by one,
The dangers that wait to assail you.
But just buckle in with a bit of a grin,
Just take off your coat and go to it;
Just start to sing as you tackle the thing
That "cannot be done," and you'll do it. —Edgar Guest[3]

---

3   In *Creating Success from the Inside Out*, p. 147.

Miracles Do Happen

Miraculous favor follows those who believe they can achieve. Has it occurred to you why you do something much better than others? You have your own unique way of doing things. This gift is your signature. It is God-given. Successful people develop their talents and skills, which sets them apart from everyone else. Listen to the voice within you. We were all born with this infinite being within us. We can even sense it without seeing it when something does not feel right. Some people call it gut feeling.

The reason some people are much better at what they do than others is because they have spent time identifying their purpose in life. They follow and develop their gifts, talents, abilities, and skills. They contact people who will help them in developing these abilities. Most of all, they listen to their infinite being for wisdom and guidance.

Most businesspeople listen to their inner voice for guidance. For example, let's say you have a business negotiation deal with a client; even though everything looks right on paper, listen to the voice within if you have a hunch that something is not right. Though all the paperwork looks great, if you do not listen to your inner voice and you go ahead and sign the deal, you will often find out you are in a big financial mess, and soon you will realize that you have been defrauded.

Even when everything looks perfect, the infinite being within us can direct us as to whether we are on the right path or not, if only we allow it to guide us.

CHAPTER 13

Value Your Ideas and Take Risks

Never underestimate your ideas, especially if they can satisfy human needs. Look for people who will finance your ideas. The only risks it will take will be finding out where these investors are, calling them to book an appointment, and going to meet them. How you will do this will be discussed below.

The difference between successful people and people who are not successful is that nonachievers give up after a few attempts, while successful people keep trying. Successful people are willing to take risks. They are problem solvers. They take on what life throws at them and, in doing so, they become achievers. They learn from their mistakes. Without risk, there is no change. You must leave your comfort zone to see results. Take a step toward your passion, and you will benefit yourself and all of humanity. Listen carefully to your passion your infinite identity is asking you to pursue. Pursue it! Let it become a reality. Your idea could be the next breakthrough for all of us.

An idea shoots into someone's brain. The idea is applied, and the answer we get is reality. Everything from the plane, invented by Oral and Wilbur Wright, to the electric bulb, invented by Thomas Edison, to the wheelchair was someone's idea that was given to him or her by his or her infinite identity. This was then applied to reality, which led toward great discoveries in the world, and these discoveries satisfied human needs.

For example, Benjamin Franklin discovered electricity. His discovery provided the basis of modern-day electrical technology, and the world has since then never been in darkness during the night. Without electricity, none of us can use the basic comforts, such as microwaves and other electrical gadgets, as we need to plug such gadgets into a socket so that the electricity generated can pass through the socket to make it work.

How to Find Financiers for Your Idea

If you have an idea that will benefit humanity, have you searched for entrepreneurs who will sell your idea and support you financially if you do not have enough money? You need to find people who have the finances, inform them, and demonstrate your ideas to them, and they will support you if they realize there will be a need for it. There are businesspeople who support people by financing their ideas. In the United Kingdom, there is a show called the *Dragons' Den*. The show is about strong business gurus who invest in people's ideas. They are famous in the business sector, and you can search for their names on the Internet, as they have Web sites that give you their contact details. You might not get them straightaway, but you might speak to their personal assistants, who will be able to give you the necessary information and tell you what arrangements they can make to enable you to get in touch with them. Oh yes, I know you are asking, my dear reader, "But will it take time?" Yes, maybe it will, and maybe it will not. Try it at least before you start thinking of how it will not work and how you will be ignored. Do not be afraid to contact any of them. If your dream will benefit humanity, then there will be a market for it and someone will finance it for you because he or she will be looking at it from the business point of view. If you have an idea, someone will have the finances to support you to turn it into reality.

I have a habit of asking for the topmost people in a company or organization when I need support from that company. The only thing the person answering the phone can say is yes or no, whichever the answer, I asked anyway, and most of the time, I get the information I was looking for from the topmost person. Please do not be afraid to call the "big boss." You might be surprised; it could be your lucky day, and he or she will be the one to answer the call.

Do You Know the Wealthy Businesspeople in Your Locality?

Often, you need not look too far for someone to finance your vision. You have to research and know the wealthy businesspeople in the locality in which you live, and you must gather the courage to call their offices if you have an idea worth looking at. Book an appointment with them. Take your idea with you, and demonstrate it to them. A lot of items have been invented not only for human comfort but to saves lives. Your idea might be so new that it can be discouraging to you, but you do not have to be discouraged. Provided you can explain what the benefits are for humanity, there will always be a market for it.

Some Investors May Miss Your Idea

Some investors may miss your idea and may not understand the need for it. You have to prepare for such encounters, so you will not be discouraged. If someone says no to your idea, just try somewhere else. Thomas Edison's idea of the electric bulb was misunderstood by a lot of people, who thought he was crazy and that he would never invent it because he had failed so many times in the process. Bear this in mind and never be discouraged if anyone says no to you.

"We are what we repeatedly do, excellence then is not an act but a habit." —Aristotle

Settling for success or failure is a habit.

Positive and Negative Habits

According to Brian Tracey, a well-known motivational teacher, good habits are hard to develop but easy to live with, and bad habits are easy to develop but hard to live with. This is true. It is very easy for us to develop negative habits like drinking and smoking but very hard to stop them and develop positive habits, such as maintaining our weight by not eating too much and exercising or not procrastinating.

Breaking or developing new habits can take at least twenty-one days; however, in difficult cases, breaking bad habits can take as long as a year.

Forming New Habits

Edward Thorndike, a psychologist in the 1800s, produced two "laws" of learning, which are the law of exercise and the law of effect. The law of exercise explains that repetition strengthens learning (or practice makes perfect), while the law of effect states that the effect of reward is to strengthen learning (or if it is pleasurable, it will be repeated). Thorndike found the second law to be more effective than mere repetition. I will discuss how these two laws can be applied to enable you to develop positive habits.

The Law of Exercise

This law demonstrates that whatever we do over and over again becomes a pattern, which strengthens with time and then develops into a habit. This applies to any habits we develop, positive or negative. For example, most artists who paint on a canvas become better at it the more they paint. The more we do something, the better we become at it. "Practice makes perfect."

Another example is spending money even when there is no need to. When you often buy any item you see that you think you must have, you become unable to put a stop to it and such spending becomes a habit. You end up spending on things you did not plan for, which can have an impact on your budget; the money you needed to save or invest in your idea that will generate wealth, you spent on clothes or shoes.

The Law of Effect

This law explains how reward strengthens learning, meaning if it is pleasurable, it will be repeated. For example, if you intend to break the habit of overspending by shopping when there is no need to, the best way is to promise yourself a reward that you have desired for quite some time but you have never been able to treat yourself to before. So you can say to yourself, "For this month, I will save £300.00. My target is to save for the next ten months, which will enable me to save £3,000.00, and when I save this money, I will spend £300.00 on my dream holiday, a weekend break in Spain. You can have the picture of the resort you want to go to on your wall as a reminder of your goal, which is to save, and the reward, which is the dream holiday. This will motivate you to save your money.

Five Steps for Changing Habits

1. Awareness—Be aware of your habits. What exactly is the habit? How is it affecting you? How is it affecting others? Like the example about spending, your habit can affect you and others. You will be financially challenged if you spend your money unwisely, which will not enable you to save to invest in your idea. Second, if you have a family, not being able to pay your bills and contribute to your family's physical needs because of overspending on things that you did not budget for can bring issues like arguments with your partner.

2. Wanting to change—An individual must consciously and rationally decide for himself or herself what is wrong and what should be done about it (Carl Rogers). This means that no one can change for you; you have to decide to change by breaking bad habits through a conscious effort, which could be a worthy goal. Convince yourself that the change in your habit is worth the effort involved.

3. Commitment—Be determined and ready to do whatever it takes to break bad habits to enable you to control your life for the better.

4. Consistent action—Change your habits one at a time; then take consistent daily actions to develop new positive ones. Do this one step at a time instead of trying to do it all at once and reward yourself toward changing a bad habit. Let your rewards be something that will motivate you to focus on achieving your goal by breaking your negative habits.

5. Perseverance—There will be times when you will question whether it is all worth the effort. You will possibly say to yourself that breaking bad habits is too difficult and that you are too set in your ways to change. However, you must stick to your goal. The change from a negative habit to a positive one is worth it, especially with the positive lifestyle that comes with it. It is more of a reason why you must not give up.

How to Handle Negative Thinking When Forming New Positive Habits

Negative Thoughts from Friends

Negative thinking could come from friends or people with whom you associate who have that same habit, as they will not take your decision to change your bad habits into positive ones seriously and will consciously or unconsciously invite you to places that feed your bad habits. If this is the case, you do not necessarily have to leave your friends forever, but you may need to disassociate yourself from them by turning their invitation down when they invite you to places that feed your bad habits.

I set forth the example about spending on clothes and shoes when you do not need them. If you have a friend who invites you for such shopping sprees, you just have to turn his or her invitation down. There are times when your life is more important than any friend, so when that habit can distract your focus and destroy your destiny, you need to disassociate yourself from the friends who feed your negative habits forever. For example, if you have a friend who is always inviting you to drink and you always come home drunk, it is time for you to end such a friendship before you become an alcoholic.

Little drops of water make a mighty ocean. Do not wait until a habit that could be changed gets out of hand and becomes a big problem because of you or your friends.

Meditation and Prayer

Breaking your bad habits may also require meditation and prayer. Do not underestimate these two elements; they are very effective in dealing with your negative habits. People's prayers are answered, but only if they are willing to meet God halfway by taking steps to stop those negative habits. Do not expect prayers to do it alone. You have a responsibility to play your part to enable your prayers to be effective. Prayer without the necessary steps to break your negative habits will yield no positive results.

Seeking Professional Help

A lot of negative habits like alcohol abuse and smoking can have a long-term effect on your life, which can affect your business if you are not in a position to manage your business because of them. Not only that, but how much you spend on these dependencies per week will astound you when you put it on paper. It may look like small amounts of money until you add them up. That is money you could invest in your business. Those habits can also break your focus from investing in your idea or pursuing your dream, and this is why you need to seek professional help when you find yourself in any of those situations.

There are organizations such as Alcoholics Anonymous from which people who have an alcohol dependency can seek help. There are also various "user-friendly" kits to stop smoking, such as nicotine patches, which are free when you go to any stop-smoking center. There are people who are ready to help, if only you take the steps to their offices, so why not try any of such resources today if you have alcohol or smoking dependencies?

Support from Others

You would seek support from the bank in the form of a loan or from a "mastermind" group if you joined a group of that sort to support you financially or give you advice if your business was going down, so you must treat any negative habits like alcohol, drug, or smoking dependencies the same way. When you join the clubs listed here or seek professional help, ask and look for people who also have the same issues as you do and want to make changes in their lives. Also, look for people who have overcome such dependencies and share with them your fears and concerns and how you are coping with the changes. They will in turn share their experiences with you, including what they are doing that is working and what is not working, and all these will enable you to make positive changes in breaking your negative habit.

Other Resources

Read about people who have been able to break those negative habits. Read about people who have successfully overcome the issues you are dealing with, as this will enable you to acquire the knowledge of what they did and what they avoided. You can then put it into practice to change your own negative habits. This also gives you strength because you know that you are not alone. Others have been in your situation before; they did something about it, and it worked for them. So you can also take those bold, positive steps, and it can work for you too.

Watch documentaries and listen to tapes or CDs that motivate you to develop positive habits. You can apply these steps in most if not all areas of your life if you want to see changes in certain aspects of your activities of daily living.

CHAPTER 14

You Are Responsible for Your Personal Development

To be a success, you have to be responsible for your personal development. You can use the five steps for changing habits in areas, such as finance, investing in your ideas, and business and time management, which is prioritizing your time for your activities of daily living. This will enable you to use your time wisely. It will also make you efficient in attending to your own personal life skills within a given period of time, thereby making you more disciplined. You will also have respect for time. It will make you selective in identifying the most important issues in your life that you need to pay attention to and help you in breaking negative habits such as procrastination.

"If it is God's will, I will succeed." Have you ever heard anyone say that? I hear it all the time, and it makes me wonder how some people can yield so much responsibility to God. If you do not comb your hair today, do you really expect God to do it for you? If you do not go to work, you will not get paid, and God has nothing to do with it. God always has his part to play, but you have your part to play as well. Look at it this way, God has put treasures in you in the form of your talents, but it is your responsibility to search inside yourself to find what you are good at and develop that talent.

I always say that *some of us are so busy bringing to God the petty things that we don't leave him time to solve the big problems.* Again, God has his part to play, and you have your part to play. If you sit down there hoping to get a job without making an effort, you will reap nothing. Please do not blame God.

"Do not be deceived; God is not mocked, for you reap whatever you sow." —Galatians 6:7

CHAPTER 15

Stay Positive

William James, the father of American psychology, said that we have the power to move the world through our subconscious minds. He advised us to impress the subconscious mind with positive ideas. In other words, whatever you think of will come to pass.

You can't wait for miracles, but miracles do happen if you believe. I have had the privilege of witnessing miracles time and time again.

In 1998, my brother got seriously ill. We took him to some of the best hospitals in the country, but no one could help him. Finally, we sent him to the Korle Bu Teaching Hospital, one of Ghana's biggest hospitals. Various tests and scans were done; the doctors did all they could, but to no avail. In the end, we were informed that he had a hole in his heart and other medical complications.

Mum and Dad were informed by the doctors that he had six months to live. They were distraught. They did all they could to save my brother, but it seemed that fate had other plans. My brother was discharged from the Korle Bu Teaching Hospital. He was to come home and die. As the months passed, my brother's condition deteriorated. My mum, a strong Christian woman of faith, still refused to accept his verdict of death. She fasted. She prayed daily for a miracle. She often knelt beside my brother during her prayers. She prayed for a miracle, and a miracle she got. Dear reader, slowly, my brother began to eat well and put on some weight over his bony body. He regained his strength. He began to walk and even to work. As you are reading this book, my brother today is married and has three kids. To this day, nobody understands how he got healed. He never understood it himself. My mum prayed for a miracle, and she got it.

> Truly I tell you, if you say to this mountain, "Be taken up and thrown into the sea" and if you do not doubt in your heart, but believe that what you say will come to pass, it will be done for you." —Mark 11:23

Sometimes the only answer is faith. Spiritual help will come to those who believe. If we only believe in the physical without the supernatural, we will never experience God's divine interventions in our lives.

CHAPTER 16

Manage Your Time Wisely

Successful people value time. Nonachievers waste it. If you are always going to work late, do not expect a promotion. If you are always arriving at business meetings late or postponing meetings for the slightest of reasons, do not expect contracts to fall in your lap. Successful people have no time for people who do not value time.

Be honest with your work when it comes to time. If it will take longer, let your client know that this is a long-term job.

For instance, anytime I intend to go to the salon to have my hair done, I call my hairdresser to book an appointment prior to the time I need it done. I then ask if she can see me on a particular date, as she has a lot of clients. Even if she gives me a time two weeks or a month away, I will wait because I like the way she does my hair. The issue is not all about the money but the end result of it. If she does good, quality work, she knows that I will call her again next time. If she cannot make the time, she will not lie about it and be greedy about the money, because she knows that if she does poor work, she will lose me as a client. This is how time and value of service blend together, and that is how anyone who wants to be successful in business must treat every area of the business.

Some tasks may require a short time while others take a long time. This is also true for the serious decisions in our lives. What are your priorities when you are managing your time? Do you solve the most important problems first or the nonessentials? Always do important things first. Learn how to set priorities. Let's say you are to travel for three months. What are the things in your work and your personal life that you need to attend to before you leave?

For instance, imagine someone who has two weeks to do his "A levels," and he is spending the first week watching the World Cup. What is the priority here? Is it the World Cup or the "A level" exams? He then rushes through his studies with speed because he has only one week left and he has not revised anything. Then he sits for the exam. The results come back, and he gets C and D grades and does not understand why. We have to manage our time wisely if we want to achieve our goals in life.

CHAPTER 17

Stay Informed

Despite what you may have heard, ignorance is not bliss. Ignorance is a killer. What you do not know can kill you. Your enemy can use vital information to destroy you.

Ask the lawyers. Those who are always in the know and have the current information in law practice use it to their advantage, and they most of the time win the best and most complicated cases because they made it their duty and responsibility to go the extra mile and to search for information to argue out their case. Knowing and being current with information in your area of expertise and applying it to the appropriate situation makes you a winner.

Imagine you want to travel to a certain part of South America where the Amazon rain forest, which is full of wildlife, is located. You did not set time aside to at least read a bit about the dangers. So soon you find yourself lost in a jungle. You spot a big snake and decide to go closer to get a better look. You don't know it is an anaconda, one of the largest and most powerful snakes in the world, which can weigh about 330 pounds. The anaconda has a habit of concealing itself underwater while looking for its prey, a strategy it uses to get its food quicker. It can be angered easily by any form of disturbance when it is relaxing. It can swallow an entire cow and hunts its prey by ambushing it, coiling itself around it, and crushing it. Pretty soon, you're dinner. Ignorance is not bliss! Sadly, there are plenty of anacondas in the workplace too. If you aren't ready, you won't survive. Being ignorant retards your progress for success too.

Keep Up on Technology

Don't be the one person at work who doesn't know how to use the latest operating system. Take classes whenever you can. Improving your education may help you get the next promotion or your dream job.

CHAPTER 18

Morality

Your moral obligation does not start and end with your family. It extends to your work and to the laws of your country. You have a moral obligation to behave yourself and function as a successful individual in society.

Listen, my dear reader, we all make mistakes, but some mistakes can be very costly. The words "I am sorry" alone won't be enough. Life is about making the right decisions and choices. There is always a price to pay for your conduct; you are responsible for your actions. Develop good moral standards to protect not only your job but your life. If you work well with your qualifications and adhere to the moral obligations relating to your work, you will be rewarded; if not, you will be responsible for your irresponsible actions.

CHAPTER 19

Communication

Communication skills are vital in our daily lives. We communicate with one another by using verbal communication—which is comprised of the words we use; the pace, pitch, intonation, and volume of our voices; variation of the choices of our words; and pauses—listening skills, and nonverbal communication, which includes our body language. Everything mentioned above plays an important part in effective communication.

Professor Albert Mehrabian, a consultant and emeritus of psychology at UCLA, brought this to light in the 1900s in establishing our understanding of body language and nonverbal communication.

Professor Mehrabian writes that there are three kinds of communication: spoken, paralinguistic, and nonverbal. During communication,

- Seven percent of the message pertaining to feelings and attitudes is in the words that are spoken
- Thirty-eight percent of the message pertaining to feelings and attitudes is paralinguistic (the way that the words are said)
- Fifty-five percent of the message pertaining to feelings and attitudes is in the facial expressions

I am going to explain these three forms of communication and also present examples in the form of scenarios so that you will have a clear understanding of what I am about to explain. Seven percent of the message pertaining to feelings and attitudes is in the words that are spoken. The words you use and your style of communication with someone can have an impact on the person's feelings positively or negatively, and this can affect his or her mood or work performance.

Scenario A

Assuming your colleague at work has made an error in the process of a task, you can set good standard of practice by saying to the person in a calm tone of voice, "I also made mistakes when I started in this new role. Let me show you how I tackled this task when I encountered it." You then demonstrate how you solved the problem to complete the task effectively. With this form of communication, you have not only mentored your colleague by letting him or her observe what a good standard of practice is and how to do a particular task, but the way in which you did so will not make him or her feel so bad. You also demonstrated that it is all right to make mistakes during the learning process, which will make the person feel that you have not only embraced the positives but the negatives and you have the understanding to put him or her on the right track. This will help that person have the clear perspective that he or she is not being criticized or picked on but is being involved and that his or her colleagues have a genuine interest in him or her and care about what that person does. This will encourage your colleague to do that task or any other task much better the next time.

Scenario B

On the flip side of this scenario, you could have also gone to your colleague and said in an aggressive or even a quiet but chilling tone, "What are you doing? Look at what you have done! Did you not have an induction on this? Do you have to be taught every single thing? Leave it. Just leave it." By tackling the issue this way, with the words you used, not only have you denied that person the chance to learn how to do a particular new task in an appropriate manner, you have made him or her reliant on others, as he or she will not be able to do that task if it resurfaces. This person will be looking for someone else to do it because you never gave him or her a chance to try it, nor did you demonstrate how the task is done. In so doing, you have made it clear to your colleague that he or she will never be able to do it. The person will also lose confidence in his or her ability to complete any task again and will be panicking when faced with a new task because he or she is afraid of being told off if he or she makes mistakes. This can prevent the person from trying any new task.

Looking at these two scenarios above, which communication skills do you think will affect the person's feelings and attitude in a positive way and will help him or her to feel motivated to put more effort into the work, do his or her best, or try some new task when the need for it arises? It will definitely be those presented in the first scenario.

Thirty-eight percent of the message pertaining to feelings and attitudes is paralinguistic (the way in which the words are said).

The way you say your words when communicating with others gives a lot of information and signals to the receivers as to what you really meant. They will decode or interpret that information depending on the way the words are said. To them, the message is not mere words but your inner thoughts and feelings.

Looking at both scenarios above, you can see that the way the words are said can have an impact on the receiver's feelings and attitudes. In the first scenario, the communication that took place between the mentor and the staff member who made the error in his or her work was positive and encouraging. The one demonstrating how the task must be done spoke to the person in a calm tone of voice in this case, whereas in the second scenario, he or she used an aggressive or calm but chilling tone of voice, which can generate a negative attitude in the person at the receiving end. In both cases, whether that person will try another new task again depends on how the words are said.

Scenario C

Another possible scenario is you saying to another person in a very quiet but chilling tone of voice, "Do not ever do that again." That can be very frightening to that individual. He or she will not do the action again; however, the person would also not want to do anything else at all just to avoid upsetting you. If such a person is not told that it is what they did that you did not like and not him or her as a person—in this case it is the "action" you are upset about and not the "actor"—the probable result of this will be that he or she will take it personally and will become withdrawn. In this scenario, it is not the mistake the person made that will stop him or her from trying anything ever again so as not to upset you, but the way you spoke to him or her.

And 55 percent of the message pertaining to feelings and attitudes is in the facial expressions. Our facial expressions expose so much of what we are thinking to others and affect the message we send to them. After we "encode" or program information and send that information to other people, they also "decode" and interpret it according to the way they saw our face through their own perception of what that meant.

Most facial expressions and other forms of communication can be misinterpreted by those receiving that information or watching an individual's body language. That is why you have to be very clear in your form of communication about what messages you are sending to your receivers and understand the way in which they communicate.

Now looking at scenario A with regard to the percentages of the message being sent from the words spoken (7 percent) and through paralinguistic channels (38 percent), the person demonstrating how the task must be done using the calm approach with a calm face and an understanding body posture to the person receiving that information will make that person relax and concentrate on what is being taught while the paralinguistic cues being sent in scenarios B and C will make that person edgy, tearful, withdrawn, or angry at being spoken to like that even though he or she made an error. In scenario B, even though the person is taught how to do the task, he or she will lose concentration because such facial expressions create a stifling atmosphere.

I always say that *sometimes it is not what was said that matters but how it was said.*

Communication involves the way we talk, how we say the words, the meaning we apply to the words, and how our body language corresponds to what we are saying.

Let's apply this to your professional life. When you are at work, for example, do you appeal to authority or do you confront authority? Assuming you have some concerns and you want to have a word with your manager about them, how do you go about it? Do you look for the right time? Remember that appealing to authority does not mean that you are weak; rather, this conciliatory approach gives your boss the impression that you are a seasoned professional.

If you do have to confront a boss or colleague, don't ever lose your composure. Don't let your face contort or your body tense up. Be calm but forceful.

Be a Good Listener

Have you ever had the experience of talking with someone who is barely paying attention to you? Maybe this person is multitasking or thinking of what she will cook for dinner. How annoying is that? How did it make you feel? Don't do that to someone else. Have an open heart too. Learn to listen to what someone has to say without being judgmental. Sometimes people just need to share and don't expect you to solve their problems or even agree with what they are saying. You just do not have to do anything but listen.

- Listen without overtalking the person.
- Listen without interrupting at every opportunity. Interrupting discourages people from talking. You give them the impression that you know much better than they do, you already know what they are about to say, or you just do not value what they are saying. Interrupt only when there is the need to do so. Listen, give them time to raise their concerns or finish what they are saying, and then ask questions relating to what they have just said. If you do not get something they said, rephrase the question by saying, "If I am hearing correctly, what you are saying is that …" Use verbal cues like "hmm," "okay," "is it?" and "right" during the conversation. This gives them the impression that you are listening to what they are saying and that you value them as people because you have shown interest in their conversation.
- Allow a caller to speak first. Let callers speak first when they call. You listen first before you share your contributions or concerns. This may seem as if it is nothing, but how many times has a friend or a work colleague called you at work to get information and you started narrating your issues, not allowing him or her to discuss the reason for the call? The person may not say anything, but he or she will not be pleased. The one who is bold enough to remind you he called you first because he has concerns so you should

allow him to speak first will then appear rude, but in reality, you did not show that you care about what he had to say.

The following section contains some points on becoming an active listener.

Becoming an Active Listener

Pay attention.
- Give the speaker your undivided attention and acknowledge the message.
- Consider the nonverbal cues you are giving to your listener.
- Look at the speaker directly.
- Put aside distracting thoughts. Don't mentally prepare a rebuttal!
- Avoid being distracted by environmental factors.
- "Listen" to the speaker's body language.
- Refrain from side conversations when listening in a group setting.

Show that you are listening.
- Use your own body language and gestures to convey your attention.
- Nod occasionally.
- Smile and use other facial expressions.
- Note your posture and make sure it is open and inviting.
- Encourage the speaker to continue with small verbal comments like "Yes," and "Uh-huh."

Provide Feedback
Our personal filters, assumptions, judgments, and beliefs can distort what we hear. As a listener, your role is to understand what is being said. This may require you to reflect what is being said and ask questions.

- Reflect what has been said by paraphrasing. "What I'm hearing is …" and "Sounds like you are saying …" are great ways to reflect back.
- Ask questions to clarify certain points like "What do you mean when you say …" "Is this what you mean?"
- Summarize the speaker's comments periodically.

Try using the "sandwich method." Let me explain. When you are making a ham sandwich, you take two slices of bread and put your ham in the middle. The bread areas are softer than the ham. Assuming I want to address issues relating to poor writing skills with a staff member during his or her supervision, I always start by giving the staff member the opportunity to speak what is on his or her mind and suggest how best we can find solutions to it. I will then come with my agenda by starting with the top of the "bread" by praising the person's strengths where his or her tasks are concerned. "I like the skills you showed when supporting Mr. A. to learn how to cook lasagna the other day," I might say. Then I'll add that this worker might also want to write down an activity plan on how he got Mr. A. to contribute to his cooking so that other staff members can use this information when they need to support Mr. A.

Then I come to the "ham" bit, which is the hard area. That's the issue I want to address. I explain that I have been reading what he or she has been writing and that it is not bad at all. Then I suggest that he or she would benefit from always writing the time and venue of an activity taking place in the diary. I will also offer some writing pointers and offer training in report writing. I end with another slice of "bread." I praise the staff member again.

If supervision sessions are not confrontational or intimidating, staff members will look forward to them and will be more likely to share their grievances and suggestions with you.

CHAPTER 20

Dress the Part

We communicate with the way we dress. Say someone comes to talk to you about a business proposition. This person's clothes are in tatters. You will try with all your heart to listen, but you will be unable to stop yourself from judging. What sort of business is this that prevents this person from buying decent clothes? It can't be very successful, can it? Learn to "walk the talk." If you dress well, you will inspire confidence in other people. If you wear a hoodie and your jeans are nearly falling from your waist, do not be surprised if someone thinks you're a thug.

CHAPTER 21

Know Yourself

I have seen people with the potential to become very good managers who may never succeed because they don't believe they can achieve this goal. They just cannot see themselves or imagine themselves occupying a position of authority. The word is too big for them. When I prompt them to apply, they say they are "waiting for the right time" or "need to learn more" before applying. They tell me they are afraid to fail and they don't want to let me down. How can you learn from an experience you have never had? You need to be in that position, to get inducted and practice constantly to get the experience. It is like running for the office of president of your country—where will you get that experience of being president before you are elected president? It isn't possible. You can't be prepared for everything. You just have to jump in and *try*! Because of their fear of failure, they stay where they are and never develop toward career success. Our perception really is our reality.

> "They always say that time changes things, but you actually have to change them yourself."
> —Andy Warhol

Maybe you will not be able to set a world record, but your urgency toward your own personal development can propel you to success so that you will have enough wealth to touch a soul and make the world a better place for at least one person.

"Can-do" people always become achievers. Can-do people rewrite history. Look at Barack Obama. Not in a million years did any African American think that a black man would be president of the United States so soon. During the 2008 campaign, there were all sorts of views on television about why a black man couldn't win. Everyone said that America was not ready for a black president. How wrong they were! Barack Obama believed in his dream and campaigned fervently to the last day. He said, "Yes, we can!" and he did. He is an inspiration to us all. So, what's your excuse for not committing to your dream and doing everything possible to achieve it? As Norman Vincent Peale once wrote, "You can if you believe you can."

I have had my fair share of painful experiences while trying to make it in this country, but I never gave up. I am a first-generation immigrant who came to Britain in the year 2000 with only £20.00 in my purse. I will never say to you that I had it easy, but I have managed to make a living, to send myself to school, and to rise through the ranks of my profession. Through hard work and perseverance, I am where I am today. I saw opportunities all around. When you come from a third-world country and you have seen hardship before, you cherish every blessing God puts on your doorstep. I am a living testimony that miracles do exist if you look for them and work hard. Please do not give up on yourself.

May this book be a blessing unto you. May it liberate your mind so you can take the steps to build a better life for yourself. I wish you Godspeed.

INSPIRATIONAL QUOTES

"Success seems to be connected with action. Successful men keep moving. They make mistakes, but they don't quit." —Conrad Hilton in *Creating Success from the Inside Out*.

"Don't feel entitled to anything you didn't sweat and struggle for." —Marian Wright Edelman in *Creating Success from the Inside Out*.

"Go to the ant, you lazybones; consider its ways, and be wise." —Proverbs 6:6

"Bloom where you are planted."   Robert Schuller in *Creating Success from the Inside Out*.

"You will never reach the palace talking like a peasant." —Mike Murdock in *One Minute Businesswoman's Devotional*.

"Temper justice with mercy." —William Shakespeare in *The Merchant of Venice*.

"If wishes were horses, beggars could ride." —Anonymous

"If you think you can do something, that's confidence. If you can do it that's competence. Both are needed for success." —John Maxwell in *The Difference Maker*.

"You are snared by the utterance of your lips; caught by the words of your mouth." —Proverbs 6:2, NRSV

"Ask and it shall be given unto you." —Matthew 7:7, NRSV

"Remember this, when you come here, what you see here, what you hear here, when you leave here, let it stay here or don't come back here." —Jamaican saying

"To everything there is a season, a time for every purpose under heaven." —Ecclesiastes 3:1, NKJV

"Wisdom is the principal thing; therefore get wisdom; and with all thy getting get understanding." —Proverbs 4:7, KJV

"My great concern is not whether you have failed, but whether you are content with your failure." —Abraham Lincoln in *Creating Success from the Inside Out*.

"We are what we repeatedly do; excellence then is not an act but a habit." —Aristotle

"Do not be deceived; God is not mocked, for you reap whatever you sow." —Galatians 6:7, NRSV

"What is impressed in the subconscious is expressed." —Dr. Joseph Murphy in *The Power of Your Subconscious Mind*.

"Truly I tell you, if you say to the mountain, 'Be taken up and thrown into the sea' and if you do not doubt in your heart, but believe that what you say will come to pass, it will be done for you." —Mark, 11:23, NRSV.

"They always say that time changes things, but you actually have to change them yourself." —Andy Warhol in *The Difference Maker*.

References and Suggested Reading

"Anaconda." Amazon Rain Forest. http://www.amazon-rainforest.org/fauna.html (accessed on July 14, 2010).

"Anaconda Snake." http://www.manbir-online.com/snakes/anaconda.htm (accessed on July 14, 2010).

Aristotle. Arisotle Quotes. Thinkexist.com. http://thinkexist.com/quotation/we_are_what_we_repeatedly_do-excellence_then-is/12820.html (accessed on August 25, 2010).

"Becoming an Active Listener." *Mind Tools—Essential Skills for an Excellent Career.* http://www.mindtools.com/CommSkll/ActiveListening.htm (accessed on July 15, 2010).

"Elisha and the Widow Story." 2 Kings 4:1–6. The Holy Bible, New King James Version. Nashville, TN: Thomas Nelson, Inc., 1990.

"Failures of Abraham Lincoln." School of Champions. http://www.school-for-champions.com/history/lincoln_failures.htm (accessed on July 14, 2010).

"Harry Potter." *J. K. Rowling Biography.* http://www.essortment.com/all/jkrowlingbiogr_reak.htm (accessed on July 14, 2010).

Holy Bible (The), King James Version. Belgium: Broadman & Holman Publishers, 1996.

Holy Bible (The), New King James Version. Nashville, TN: Thomas Nelson Inc., 1990.

Holy Bible (The), New Revised Standard Version. Nashville, TN: Thomas Nelson, Inc., 1989.

Maxwell, John, ed. *The Difference Maker.* Nashville, TN: Thomas Nelson, Inc., 2006.

Mehrabian, Albert. *Mehrabian's Communication Research.* http://www.businessballs.com/mehrabiancommunications.htm (accessed on July 14, 2010).

Murdock, Mike. *One Minute Businesswoman's Devotional.* The Wisdom Centre, Texas, 1992.

Shakespeare, William. *The Merchant of Venice.* In *The Illustrated Stratford Shakespeare.* London: Chancellor Press, 1982.

Murphy, Joseph, Dr. *The Power of Your Subconscious Mind.* United Kingdom: Parker Publishing, 1988.

Taylor, Ephren W., and Emerson Brantley, eds. *Creating Success from the Inside Out.* New Jersey: John Wiley & Sons, Inc., 2008.

Thorndike, Edward. "The Law of Exercise and the Law of Effect." *Psychology: A Graphic Guide to Your Mind and Behaviour.* Edited by Nigel C. Benson. Cambridge, UK: Icon Book Ltd., 2007.

Tracey, Brian. "Breaking Bad Habits" in "Five Simple Steps for Changing a Habit." Ezine @rticle. http://ezinearticles.com/?Breaking-Bad-Habits-5Simple-Steps-for-Changing-a-habit&id=71021 (accessed on July 14, 2010).

Rogers, Carl. "Rogerian Therapy—Person Centered Therapy." *Psychology: A Graphic Guide to Your Mind and Behaviour*. Edited by Nigel C. Benson. Cambridge, UK: Icon Book Ltd., 2007.

Varah, Chad. "Why the Samaritans Started." *The Samaritans*. http://www.samaritans.org/about_samaritans/introduction_to_samaritans/why_samaritans_started.aspx (accessed on July 7, 2010).